Common Sense Business for Kids

by Kathryn Daniels

published by
Bluestocking Press
www.BluestockingPress.com

Printed and bound in the United States of America
Cover by Brian C. Williams, El Dorado, CA
Edited by Jane A. Williams
Additional content editing by Ann M. Williams

Library of Congress Cataloging-in-Publication Data

Daniels, Kathryn Ann.
    Common sense business for kids / by Kathryn Daniels.
        p. cm.
    Includes index.
    Summary: "Using practical judgment derived from experience rather than study, and using real-world examples, Anthony Maybury explains common sense realities behind basic business principles, including: fixed and variable costs, market potential, research, price strategies, inventory management, salesmanship, and management techniques. Discusses characteristics needed to be a successful entrepreneur, manager, or employee" --Provided by publisher.
    ISBN-13: 978-0-942617-61-0 (alk. paper)
    ISBN-10: 0-942617-61-4 (alk. paper)
    1. Business--Juvenile literature. 2. Management--Juvenile literature. I. Title.

HF5381.2.D36 2006
658--dc22

                                              2006013189

Contents

Contents

Quantity Discounts Available

Bluestocking Press books are available at special quantity discounts for bulk purchases to individuals, businesses, schools, libraries, and associations.

For terms and discount schedule contact:

Special Sales Department
Bluestocking Press
Phone: 800-959-8586
email: CustomerService@BluestockingPress.com
web site: www.BluestockingPress.com

Specify how books are to be distributed: for classrooms, as gifts, as premiums, as fund raisers, or to be resold.

About Kathryn Daniels

Kathryn Daniels was born in Sacramento, California. After earning degrees in Cecchetti ballet from the International Society of Teachers of Dancing, Ms. Daniels attended college and graduated top of her class with a Bachelor's degree in Business Administration/Marketing. She continued on to earn a Master's degree in Liberal Arts. Ms. Daniels is the author of several study guides for the Uncle Eric books, published by Bluestocking Press.

About Anthony Joseph Maybury

Anthony Joseph Maybury was born in Hamilton, Ohio in 1923. In 1943, he married the love of his life, Ruth, and they raised four children together. (Their son, Richard J. Maybury, is the author of the Uncle Eric books, published by Bluestocking Press.) In 1959, the Mayburys moved to California to provide their children with more affordable educational opportunities.

In his career, Mr. Maybury progressed from shoe-shine boy to a prestigious position as the Western regional sales manager for a major coffee company. His diverse experiences in the business world led him to amass a wealth of "common sense" to share with others. Mr. Maybury was so successful that he was able to take early retirement at the age of fifty-five.

Since retiring, Mr. Maybury has enjoyed volunteering in various organizations, traveling, and spending time with his children and grandchildren.

Preface

This book is a collaboration between myself and Anthony Joseph Maybury. I wrote this book after Mr. Maybury shared with me his experiences, wisdom, and "common sense" insights about business.

Throughout the process of writing this book, I had the pleasure of attending many meetings with Mr. Maybury. There was very little formality in these wonderful conversations. Instead, Mr. Maybury shared dozens of stories about his experiences in the business world. His warmth, zeal, humor, and compassion constantly impressed me, as did his genuine love and concern for future generations and his desire to see young people find meaningful, satisfying work in the world. I hope I have been able to capture some of Mr. Maybury's remarkable spirit in his stories that I retell throughout this text.

To the best of my ability, I have recounted Mr. Maybury's stories, anecdotes, and wisdom faithfully. Occasionally, and with Mr. Maybury's permission, I have inserted knowledge I learned from my business school education. This combination is meant to provide you with a book largely filled with the common sense you won't usually find in traditional business textbooks, while also providing a glimpse into what a traditional business education might offer.

While I learned many valuable things in business school, nothing has resonated with me more deeply (or had so great an impact on my personal outlook regarding the business world) than Mr. Maybury's common sense insights about business.

—Kathryn Daniels

1

Business: It's All About Common Sense

What does it take to be successful in business? Anthony Maybury used to think that in order to be successful one must know how to put complex theories into practice. He thought success required knowledge of advanced mathematics, inventory management equations, and whiz-bang marketing techniques. But he made some interesting discoveries.

In the pages that follow, Mr. Maybury shares these discoveries with readers.

• • •

My dictionary defines common sense as sound practical judgment derived from experience rather than study. And that's exactly what this book is going to be about. Everything I talk about will be "common sense"—my common sense. It's knowledge that I've acquired through years of experience. Some of the experiences happened to me, some happened to my friends and co-workers. But it took a long time to gain these experiences. When you're young, you don't have many experiences in your repertoire, so it's often helpful to look to the experiences of others when you are about to embark on new journeys of your own so that, hopefully, your experiences will be positive ones.

I began my journey in business in my hometown, a small town in Ohio. I was a teenager in the 1930s and back then it was much easier for young people to find work than it is today.

I got my first job in a shoe-shine shop, shining shoes. Then I worked in a hardware store, stocking shelves. These were small ventures, but I learned a great deal just by observing my bosses, our customers, and the successes and failures of the businesses.

I married my high school sweetheart, served in World War II, then came home and started a family and got a new job.

There was little in my youth that "prepared" me for success in business and, when I returned from the war, I had no opportunity to attend college. Yet, by the early 1960s, I had become the Western regional sales manager for one of America's major commercial coffee companies. Eventually, I became West coast general manager (which was considered a very high position in the company) and was successful enough to retire early at the age of fifty-five.

How did I succeed?

I had ambition, and I appreciated common sense.

Growing up during the Great Depression, I knew what it was like to do without, and I knew what it meant to work hard. I was willing to work hard to make a better life for my family and myself and I kept my mind open to learn everything I could in every situation that presented itself—and I tried to adapt what I learned to business situations. I realize this now because I can look back on my experiences and choices and see them with the clarity of hindsight. But I wasn't always so sure of how to go about things, especially when I was just starting out in the business world.

I remember the day I was asked to become the Western regional sales manager for my company; I was excited, but I was also a little scared. After all, I was still this guy from small-town Ohio, without any college degrees or "expertise" in business. I thought there must be some *secret* to success in "big business" that I didn't know. And I wanted to know the secret. I wanted to be prepared to take on my new job, to be the best that I could be. So I asked my new boss, "What does it take to be successful in business?"

His answer? "Common sense!"

Well, I just didn't think that was enough. I mean, didn't *everybody* have common sense? If that's all it took to be successful in business, why were so many people failing? No, there *had* to be another answer. I wanted another opinion on the subject.

So, I got a meeting with one of the big executives in my company. I spent several days shadowing him, listening to him. And I asked him my burning question: "What does it take to be successful in business? What is the secret?"

He said, "There's no secret. It just takes good common sense—and confidence in yourself."

And I came to see that they were right. And I also came to see that common sense is not so "common," after all. In fact, common sense needs explaining.

What *is* common sense?

Should automobile manufacturers start putting square wheels on cars?

Should a person go to the supermarket to buy milk if they don't have any money to pay for it?

Should a person wear a heavy parka to the beach in Hawaii?

Should a child try to sell ice cold lemonade on a snowy winter day?

No.

Square wheels won't roll.

You can't buy milk if you don't have a means to pay for it.

You'd be more than a little uncomfortable wearing a winter coat on a warm, sunny beach.

And a child would be more successful selling a hot beverage on a snowy winter day than ice cold lemonade.

That's just common sense, right?

But it goes deeper than that.

Many people think they have common sense—but they don't. And really, when it comes down to it, they just don't *think*. That's where their problems come in.

It doesn't take a genius to know that you should wear a jacket when it's cold—that's just common sense. But what if someone had lived in Hawaii all their life and wasn't familiar with a climate like Alaska's? In Alaska, it's very cold in January. In Hawaii, it's warm in January. If the Hawaii resident packed for a trip to Alaska in January without *thinking*, or without researching, he would feel that it's common sense to pack shorts and t-shirts and swimsuits. But he'd be mighty sorry when he arrived in Alaska and discovered his mistake. Sure, he'd know better next time. But the problem with business is that mistakes are often so costly there can't *be* a "next time." So, you have to think things through *first*.

To succeed in business you need to be observant about yourself and about the world around you.

First of all, understand yourself, your strengths, your weaknesses, your interests, your goals. We all have something to contribute to the world and many of us use business as the vehicle to get our contributions into society. Through observation and introspection, you can determine what needs exist in society and which of these you can help fill and how business might help you do that. Even if you pursue formal education, you will need to merge it with common sense—and common sense comes from experience and observation.

Business courses in college may help you learn some of the mechanics of business operations and these can be helpful in running a business, but never forget that business is really organic.

Sometimes it is easy to imagine business in a very detached way, like it's a giant machine somehow operating on its own. I encourage you to remember that business is fundamentally about people—people buying and selling things to make their lives better. If you think about business from this perspective, it is much easier to view business as "common sense" rather than as something complicated and abstract.

I don't pretend to be an "expert"—I know I don't have all the answers. I'm just that guy from Ohio who discovered the "secret" to success in business—the guy who was fortunate enough to live his dream. I want you to realize your dreams, too. And I hope that, in some small way, this little book will help you get there.

Now, let's get started.

2

The Biggest Cause
of Business Failure

Just as common sense and ambition are the biggest keys to success in business, *under-capitalization* is the surest path to failure.

Capital is the buildings, office equipment, and other tools workers need to produce products/services. Capital also means the money saved to buy the buildings and equipment. It consists of both the upfront and ongoing costs of running a business. So, under-capitalization means that the person starting the business doesn't really have enough money to run the business.

For example, suppose you decide that you want to go into business selling books. You don't have much money, but you believe you'll sell enough books to pay your bills, so you go ahead and buy what you need on *credit*.[1] And maybe you do sell some books—but not nearly as many as you expected. As a result, you don't have enough money to pay off your bills. Now you've got to borrow more money—maybe from a

---

[1] When you buy on credit a company lets you take the product or service now based on the promise that you will pay later.

friend or family member or the bank—to try to pay off your initial *debt*;[2] and now you're in even more debt. And, since you've got to pay *interest*[3] on those debts, now you owe even *more*. It's a vicious cycle—and a classic example of under-capitalization.

When starting a business, you should always depend on what you have.

Having a good idea is important—without a good idea for a product or service there would be no reason to start a business. But you also need to make sure you have enough capital to start that business. You've probably heard the expression "Don't count your chickens before they've hatched"—it's the same thing in business: don't count on the income from sales until you've made those sales. Certainly you can make projections on how much you will sell (this is called *forecasting*), but you should have enough capital acquired to pay your initial bills *before* that first sale is ever made. *Depend on what you have.* And, remember, it's better to start small and grow than to risk it all right away; taking a little time and effort to reach your goals is better than never getting there at all. Starting small introduces you to experiences that you can build upon to grow your business—you will gain more and more "common sense" along the way so that when it comes time to make the decisions that will have big repercussions you'll be better equipped to make the best choices.

As a general rule, you should have about six months worth of capital "in the bank" (in reserve) *before* you start your business. Each business has unique needs, so the

---

[2] Debt. Your obligation to pay what you owe.

[3] Interest is the price paid for the use of money.

estimate may vary, but it's a good idea to have enough capital in reserve to keep you going for a few months, considering you might not make as much money as you hoped to make right away. Six months reserve is the common standard. Sometimes it takes longer than you would like in order to begin making *profit*.[4] Often, it takes a few months for people to become aware that your business exists and to become familiar and comfortable with the idea of buying your products/services. If your business isn't wildly successful right away, that doesn't necessarily mean it won't be successful eventually. But, you need to be able to support yourself and the business while you wait for that "eventually" to happen— otherwise, you might go broke before you even have a chance to succeed. Again, six months capital in reserve is a good guideline.

------

[4] Profit. The result of selling products or services for more than the cost of producing them.

3

Operating Costs:
There is More to Business Than
What You Pay for the Product

Understanding *start-up costs* and *operating costs* is another important component to success in business, and it corresponds nicely with the idea of capital (and under-capitalization).

Start-up costs are those required to open the business; operating costs are those that the business demands on an ongoing basis.

Many years ago, I knew a fellow who wanted to start a restaurant business. He came to me full of enthusiasm with dreams of wealthy success. You see, he figured he could sell coffee for about fifteen cents per cup and that he could make coffee for three cents per cup! "That's *twelve cents profit* per cup!" he told me gleefully.

"How do you figure the coffee will only cost you three cents per cup?" I asked him.

"Simple," he replied. And he did a little math about the cost of one pound of coffee beans and the number of cups of coffee he could make out of one pound of beans and, *voila,* the cost came to three cents per cup.

I was in a tough position. I didn't want to dash my friend's hopes, but I also didn't want to see him go bankrupt. It was clear he hadn't considered all the start-up costs involved.

I figured the kindest thing was to reveal a little more of the big picture to him. I told him that, yes, the *coffee* itself might cost three cents per cup. But, how much did the cups cost? How about the napkins? The cream? The sugar? What about the expense of purchasing the coffee maker? How many cups of coffee would he have to sell to pay for the *overhead*: the cost for electricity to run the coffee maker and lights and cash register, the rent for the building, the insurance, employees' wages? Adding all those costs up, it would have actually cost my friend *more* than fifteen cents to "make" one cup of coffee.

By ignoring all the start-up and operating costs, instead of making twelve cents *profit* on each cup of coffee, my friend would have actually *lost* money.

Again, this comes back to the concept of common sense and thinking through an idea. My friend, although very intelligent, was blinded by the idea of huge profits and had tunnel vision when it came to looking at "the big picture" of starting a business.

I didn't reveal a big secret to him. If he had simply stopped and thought about what is required to make a cup of coffee in his own home he would have realized the same thing—it takes more than a one pound bag of coffee beans to make coffee!

Always remember, *there is more to business than what you pay for the material product.*

4

Market Potential:
Two Isn't Always Better Than One

Let's say you have started your own business—a retail store—and that business is terrific. It's all you could have hoped for—and more. You are making lots of sales. More importantly, you're making a hefty *profit*. Let's say you're making $50,000 profit per year.

Should you open a second store? Just think of it. If you made $50,000 per year in profit with *one* store, couldn't you make $100,000 per year by opening that second store?

$50,000 + $50,000 = $100,000. Right?

Mathematically, yes. In the business world, probably not.

Again, we have to look at the big picture. We have to look at the issues of capital, start-up costs, and operating costs. And we have to look at *market potential.* In other words, do you have enough money to open another store? Can you pay for a second rent, more inventory, more employees? And, even if you can, *will you have enough customers to make it worthwhile*?

Make sure growth opportunities will be worth all the extra time, energy, and expense involved.

Market potential is a big, fancy word used in business. It sounds complicated and mysterious. But, again, there are no secrets.

Let's say you opened your store in a small town—you're the first ballet boutique in the area. ABC Ballet Academy is the only dance studio in the town and they have fifty students enrolled in ballet classes. The parents of all the ballet dancers from ABC Ballet Academy come to your shop to buy tu-tus and leotards and tights and slippers for their kids. Would it be wise to open another shop in your town? Would you double your profits?

Probably not, unless attendance at ABC Ballet Academy suddenly doubles or another dance studio opens—and maybe not even then. Consider, if there are only fifty potential ballet students in your town, then you can only hope to have about fifty customers for your store. If you open another store, you may have doubled the inventory but you will still have only fifty customers.

The above example is an illustration of market potential. In your town your market consists of the parents of fifty ballet students, this is your target market, your potential customer base. It is highly unlikely that anybody else in town would be interested in purchasing children's ballet attire. If you are the only ballet boutique in town, you have 100% of the potential market—in other words, if a dancer needs ballet slippers, his or her parent(s) will buy from you. If you open another ballet boutique, you will still have 100% of the market—but it will be split between your stores (in other words, why bother with another store if you won't get any more customers?). Also, if someone *else* opens a ballet boutique in your town, your potential market could switch (in whole or in part) to the competition. You probably won't be able to hold onto 100% of the market anymore. Some of your customers might stop buying from you and start buying from your competitor. You will need to come up with new strategies to try to retain your customer base.

Now let's look at the example from another point of view. In this case, you have just moved to the small town. You notice that there is a dance studio called ABC Ballet Academy, as well as a retail store that sells dance clothing and supplies. Right now, that dance boutique has 100% of the market. But you'd like to start a dance supply store, too. So, the question is: *how much of the market can you get?* 10 percent? 50 percent? 75 percent?

You have to *research* your market—before you ever open your store—to see whether you will reach enough of the potential market to be successful. In other words, will there be enough people willing to buy *your* product? We'll talk more about market research a little later on, but for now let's stay with market potential.

I observed a real-life example of market potential when I first moved to California. Another major coffee company, one of our competitors, wanted to break into the West coast market with instant coffee. They thought they could reach 70% of the coffee market—that is, they believed that 70% of all coffee drinkers would buy their instant coffee. But they hadn't done any research! At that time, instant coffee was only 6% of the total coffee market—so, even if this company could tap into 100% of the instant coffee market (which would be a pretty unrealistic assumption) they would still get only 6% of the total coffee market. They ended up realizing their mistake before it was too late—but if they had gone through with their business venture on the idea that they would tap into 70% of the total coffee market, they would most certainly have gone bankrupt.

Again, this was a lack of common sense. It seems only natural that not everyone will want to buy the same product. Think of your family and friends and the types of foods and beverages in your kitchens. You probably all have some sort of breakfast cereal, juice, snacks, something for dessert—but it's highly unlikely that all of you have the exact same type of cereal, juice, snacks, or dessert in your house. Maybe some of you even have more than one type of cereal in your cupboard because different family members like different kinds of cereal. So, just by using common sense and observation you can see that no *one* cereal company should hope to capture *every* cereal-eater in the country, that just wouldn't be logical, because not everyone has the same taste in cereal.

5

More About Markets:
The Perfect Fit

Remember when we talked about the tourist packing a heavy jacket for a trip to the warm, sunny beach in Hawaii? That seemed like a pretty unnecessary garment to bring to the beach—after all, it's just common sense that you wouldn't wear something like that in hot weather.

So, do you think a businessperson would be wise to set up a shop on the beach in Hawaii specializing in fine-quality wool overcoats?

That would probably not be very profitable. Even if you had no competition (no other shops in the area selling wool overcoats) it is very unlikely enough people would buy from you—lack of competition doesn't mean you'll sell something, people still have to want to buy what you have to sell. In this case, it would be much better to sell swimsuits or sunscreen or an ice-cold beverage—because that's what people on the beach in Hawaii want to buy!

After all, it's just *common sense*.

However, you'd be surprised by how many big businesses don't pay attention to what the customer really wants. They try to get the market to fit a product (which generally doesn't work), rather than finding a product to fit the market (which usually does work).

For example, imagine that every youngster in the country eats fruit for a snack because it is good for them. In this example, let's say that 95% of kids don't like bananas, and that 100% of kids do like oranges. However, the people who design the marketing campaign for a large fruit company decide that they like bananas best of all the fruits, so that's what they focus their advertising campaign around—a big, dancing banana. They start farms to mass-produce bananas in anticipation of the demand that will start pouring in from people who see the ad. They think that anybody who sees the ad will want to eat bananas. Naturally, the ad will not change the minds of most of the kids in our example who already know they dislike bananas. Those kids will still prefer oranges and they will go some place where they can get oranges. Even if a few kids are intrigued by the advertisement and are interested in trying the bananas, once they taste them they will likely discover that they still don't like bananas and will want to go back to oranges. The fruit company did not bother checking into their market first (researching kids' food preferences) to see what the customers (the kids in our example) truly wanted to eat. If they had, they could have designed their advertising campaign and production schedule to sell oranges (a product that the kids in our example want) rather than bananas (a product that most kids in our example don't want) and would probably have made more money and had a lot of happy customers. Instead, they lost money because they tried to convince the kids in our example to buy something they did not want, rather than giving them what they did want.

I'll now provide a real-life example from my experience working in the coffee company. On the East coast, to make a 12-cup pot of coffee, people used three ounces of coffee—East-coasters liked a good, strong cup of coffee. When my company came to the West coast, however, we found that people there only used *two-and-a-half* ounces of coffee to make a 12-cup pot—West-coasters liked a nice, light cup of coffee. So, what did our company do? *We tried to change the customers' mind*—but it didn't work, and we almost went broke in the process. We were ignoring the common sense of paying attention to what people really want!

It is very, very difficult to get people to change their minds. People like what they like. Sometimes some people argue that advertising gets people to change their minds—but it's pretty difficult to do. If you hate bananas, seeing a dancing banana in a commercial won't suddenly change your taste buds—indeed, you might even have a negative impression of the company selling the bananas because you will associate the company with something you don't like (bananas). Well, in this real-life situation, West-coasters liked a nice, light cup of coffee. A strong, dark cup of coffee tasted wrong to them. And even though our big fancy coffee company came and tried to tell them that strong, dark coffee is best, they didn't change their opinion of what sort of coffee they wanted to drink. They liked what they liked. And pretty soon our company figured out that it was better to give the customers what they wanted—and make money when they bought that product—than to lose money with a bunch of fruitless advertising targeted at trying to change the customers' minds! So, we started packaging the coffee in the amount that would appeal to the West-coast customers—that is, the coffee was sold in such a way that it was easy for the consumer to make a light cup of coffee.

Again, it is important to look at the whole picture.

Our West coast operations weren't stable yet. Sure, we were now selling the West-coasters their desired concentration of coffee, but we also distributed industrial-sized combination packages to restaurants. These contained the coffee bags, plus cream and sugar. East-coast restaurants loved this package because, on the East coast, people used lots of cream and sugar in their coffee. Well, guess what? On the West coast, people didn't use much cream or sugar—they didn't need it because they drank lighter coffee. So, why would the restaurants want to buy packages that contained cream and sugar—why pay for something their customers wouldn't use? Again, we almost went bust trying to sell something that nobody wanted! Thankfully, we were observant—and flexible: so we gave people what they wanted and, as a result, we were successful.

Observe. Know your market. When it comes to selling something, be it a product or service, you want to find the right product for the right market right away. Our coffee company was fortunate—we had enough capital to recover when we goofed. But, for many people, mistakes can mean the end of their business.

6

Research, Research, and More Research

We've discussed that it is important to *not* sell what people *don't* want to buy—or, said positively, that it is vital to sell only what people *want* to buy. We've also discussed the necessity of knowing exactly how much capital you need in order to start a business—and to be wary about spending more money than you already have.

So, the big questions are: How do you know what people want to buy? How do you know how much your business will cost you? How do you know whether it's all going to be worthwhile and profitable?

Again, there are no mysterious "secret" answers. You just have to use your common sense, the things you learn from observation and example—and you have to do a whole lot of research. It is always important to be mindful of what you need to know that you don't already know, and then find out how to acquire the knowledge. It's also important to keep in mind that business is more than a company selling a product/ service to customers—fundamentally, business involves a transaction between *people*. Sometimes the fancy business "buzz-words" and formulas and equations make people lose track of that personal aspect. Whether it's one person selling a book to another person at a garage sale, or thousands of employees selling their company's product to millions of customers nationwide, it still comes down to people (businesspersons) trying to provide other people (consumers/customers) with the product/service those consumers need or want—that they believe will make their lives better in some way.

Market research is another "buzz-word" in business. Large corporations have entire departments devoted to "market research" and hire specially trained "market analysts." But you don't have to have a degree in Marketing to be a Market Analyst. You just have to use your eyes, your ears, and your common sense.

Stated simply, market researchers (analysts) research a market to determine whether a product or service will sell in that market. Basically, a market is a group of consumers (people able and willing to buy a product). Markets exist for all sorts of things: ethnic cuisine, baby bottles, parakeet toys, 80th birthday greeting cards. Different types of people make up different markets—this is called *market demographics.* Demographics are the characteristics of a population—or segment of the population —characteristics like age, gender, marital status, level of education, and ethnicity. Markets are often broken down into demographic segments and market-ers try to target their ads to the largest segments of each market—that way, they will reach the largest number of potential buyers for the smallest cost.

Let's look at the example of the baby bottle market. Anybody who buys a baby bottle is part of the baby bottle market. A 70-year-old grandma who buys a baby bottle for her grandchild, a 25-year-old new mother who buys it for her own baby, a twelve year old boy who buys it for his baby sister because his dad asked him to. But the market researcher will try to discover which of these types of customers would be *most likely* to buy baby bottles *most often*. In this example, do you think it would be wise to target advertisements to the twelve year old big brother? No. He just bought the bottle one time as a favor for his dad. He most likely wouldn't buy one again until he becomes a father himself. It would be better to target the ads to the parents of babies, they are the ones most likely to regularly purchase baby bottles.

Usually, the same consumer is part of many different market segments at the same time. For example, let's say the 25-year-old new mother loves Thai food, has a pet parakeet, and her grandfather is having his 80th birthday. She would be part of the ethnic foods market, the parakeet toy market, the 80th birthday greeting card market, *and* the baby bottle market. Sometimes, marketers will try to dovetail their marketing efforts to target more than one area at once. For example, if research proves that most people who love Thai food also own parakeets, a Thai food manufacturer and a parakeet toys manufacturer might get together to make a special offer to their customers—for example, buy three Thai Foods Frozen Dinners and receive a free Squawky Parakeet toy; or, receive a coupon for $1 off a Thai Frozen Foods Dinner when you buy a Squawky Parakeet toy. The Squawky Parakeet company would hope to get some of the Thai Food customers and the Thai Food customers might get some of the Squawky Parakeet customers. It is considered a win-win situation because the companies are not in competition but they can share customers.

Market researchers use complicated mathematical formulas and complex computer programs to determine which markets to target. But they are simply trying to answer the same question that you want answered: *Will anybody buy the product I want to sell?*

So, let's return to our example of the guy who wants to open a business on the beach in Hawaii. What should he sell? What should his shop look like? Which type of consumer should he sell to? He could do a lot of studying and learn all the computer programs and mathematical formulas market researchers use—or he could pay a market research company to do the research for him. But, he's starting out small and he doesn't have a lot of money to spend or time to spare. Moreover, he doesn't need to launch a national or international advertising campaign. He just needs to know what his potential customers would want to buy so that he can sell it. He needs to determine whether he can afford to go into that business and whether he will make enough profit to make it worthwhile.

Who will his customers be? If he only has a retail establishment (storefront) and no mail order or Internet presence, his customers will be limited to the people who come into his store—the people who visit the beach. Probably most of them will be tourists. More specifically, they will be tourists to Hawaii. Most specifically, they will be tourists who chose to come to that particular beach in Hawaii.

What will they want to buy? Again, all the businessperson has to do is pay attention and use common sense. Well, people at the beach usually like to play in the sand. Should he sell sand? Of course not! There's lots of free sand all over the beach for people to play with, so why would consumers buy it from him? It has to be something people want to buy or need to buy. Should he sell computers? Most people need computers, right? But most people don't want to buy a computer when they are on vacation in Hawaii! These are rather absurd examples, but they are meant to help you remember the importance of pursuing careful and thorough research, keeping in mind the big picture.

Our businessperson could think about what he buys when he is a tourist—or what his friends and family buy. Then, he would realize that usually he buys things that he wants to take home as souvenirs (like a Hawaiian shirt), or things he wants to give as gifts (like a shell necklace), or things that he forgot to pack (like sunscreen). Okay, so he decides to sell souvenirs and sundry items. The sundry items are easy—film and sunscreen and snacks. But what kind of souvenirs should he sell? Again, he has to look at his environment and customers to determine that. Sometimes, people buy expensive art and jewelry for their souvenirs. But those people shop in expensive galleries and boutiques in fancy shopping districts. A $10,000 sculpture isn't something most people would buy at a beach shack. No, most people want cute or interesting "mementos" from a trip to the beach—a seashell magnet, postcards, a t-shirt. And if that's what people want to buy, that's what the businessperson should sell.

What should this store look like? A rustic mountain lodge? A Swiss chalet? A 1950s diner? Probably not. Again, our friend could hire expensive interior decorators to help with this decision, but good common sense will tell our businessperson that the ambiance of the shop should reflect the mood of the setting, the expectations of the customers, the type of items to be sold, and his budget. Probably it would have a beach or Hawaiian theme. It would be tidy and attractive, but it wouldn't have thousands of dollars worth of original paintings by Monet on the walls.

If our friend has the only shop on the beach, he doesn't have competition. But let's say there is another shop on the beach selling inexpensive Hawaiian/beach souvenirs, too. That's competition. So our friend would have to find a way to *differentiate* his shop from the competition. In other words, how will our businessperson motivate people to buy from *him* and not the other shop? There are lots of ways.

Maybe our friend will provide exceptional customer service, or lower prices, or a unique selection of products—maybe even design a sign out front that is so eye-catching people can't help stopping at his shop first.

Finding out who your customers are, what they are able and willing to buy, and discovering how to persuade them to buy your product instead of someone else's—that's market research.

After you figure out where you need to sell, what you need to sell, and to whom you need to sell, you need to do more research. This is where things like capital and fixed costs and variable costs and overhead costs come in. Again, you don't want to do any guesswork here, but you also don't need years of finance and accounting courses to figure it out. You look to your competition. You look to your own resources. Do you remember my friend who thought he could sell coffee for 15 cents per cup and make 12 cents profit per cup? He was willing to listen to my experience and advice, and thankfully this helped prevent him from making a big mistake and losing lots of money. But a lot of people just charge ahead once they get an idea, and they start building their business before they have done any research, and this leads to trouble and, often, business failure. Know your market and know your resources and capabilities—and potential for profit (or loss!) *before* you ever spend a dime.

7

How Much Does It Cost?

As we have already briefly discussed, if you have decided to go into business selling a product or service, you need to determine how much that product/service will cost. First, how much does it cost *you* to make the product or provide the service. Second, how much should it cost the customer to *buy* the product/service. Third, how much profit do you need to make for the venture to be worthwhile to you.

We have already looked at ways to determine the cost of making an item or providing a service. Do you remember my friend with the "three-cent cup of coffee?" Research is the key to properly determining the true costs of doing business—especially overhead costs that you might not originally consider. Know how much it will cost to run the entire business—not just how much it costs for the raw materials involved in making the product. All of these expenses need to be provided for if you want to make a profit.

Once you have determined how much it costs to produce the product or provide the service, you can decide how much you want to sell the product or service for. Again, you can use complex formulas. Or you can use common sense and observation.

I remember one occasion when our coffee company acquired a large grocery store account. We had a big meeting with our Chairman of the Board and a bunch of the executives from the grocery firm. The grocery executives were telling us how they did business, and they used lots of complex formulas to tell us how they determined the price they were going to charge for the coffee.

Well, I was lost in that quagmire of formulas—I'd never seen anything like it before. When we took a coffee break, the Chairman came up to me and told me not to pay any attention to the new execs. "They're just trying to sound impressive with their big, fancy equations," he told me, "But I'll tell you the way I look at it." He got out a pad of paper and a pen and wrote down his own equation. It looked like this:

$$\begin{array}{r} \$1.00 \\ +\ .25 \\ \hline \$1.25 \end{array}$$

"That's my common sense equation," he told me. "If I know something costs me $1 to produce, and I want to make 25-cents profit when I sell it, then I have to charge $1.25 for it!"

Finally, an equation that made sense to me!

Here's another example. Let's say it costs you $5 to produce a widget. It is common sense that you can't sell it for $4; you would lose $1 for every widget you sold! At the same time, if every other company is selling widgets for $4, you can't compete with them. Customers wouldn't want to buy a widget from you for $6 if they could buy a widget of comparable quality elsewhere for $4.

Unless your widget is special, if it has something *extra* that the other companies' widgets don't—something people will be willing to pay an extra $2 for. Or maybe, if you offer exceptional customer service, people will want to pay more just for the pleasure of being able to buy from you. But, again, you have to know your market. Are you selling your widgets in an upscale area where people are able and willing to spend extra money for a "fancy" widget and quality service. Or are you selling widgets in a less affluent area where people just want the basic widget and don't have the money or inclination to pay for more than a basic widget.

Make sure that people want to buy what you want to sell— for the price at which you are able and willing to sell it.

You also have to be careful that you are making the kind of profit that you *want* to make. After all, there has to be a reason why you are going through all the time and effort and risk to start your own business. Some people go into business because they want to have their dream job—and it has nothing to do with monetary profit. Those people can be very happy as long as they are making enough money to support themselves and keep the business going. Big profits don't matter to them because they are doing what makes them happy— they don't need more money to make them happier. Other people go into business because they want to make big profits—they want lots of money. The business itself isn't what makes them happy, other things make them happy and they want to make enough money so that they can pay for these "other things" that they want. And some people don't really have a choice, they have to start their own business because they need to support themselves and it is their only option. They aren't looking for a dream job or huge profits right away, just a way to make a living.

So, you have to think hard about what kind of person you are,[5] why you want to start your business, and what will make you happy. Your answers will help you understand what to sell, who to sell it to, and how much you should charge for it.

---

[5] To help you determine if you have the temperament to be an entrepreneur, read CAPITALISM FOR KIDS by Karl Hess, published by Bluestocking Press. Web site: www.BluestockingPress.com. Phone: 800-959-8586.

8

Don't Put All Your Eggs in One Basket

You've probably heard the expression "Don't put all your eggs in one basket." Well, that common sense phrase can be applied to business. Think of the eggs as sales and the basket as one of your customers: don't give the bulk of your business's sales to any one customer. That way, if the proverbial basket breaks, you won't lose all of your eggs.

Our coffee company had a policy of never letting any one customer make up more than 5% of our business. We figured that our company was large enough to handle a loss of 5% of our sales (i.e. if one of our customers stopped buying from us) and we could also handle an increase in business of 5% (if we took on a new customer) without having to build new facilities.

Just as you have to consider that the people who buy from you might go out of business (or lose their source of income), you have to consider that your customer could put *you* out of business if they make up too large a portion of your business.

Here's an example. Let's say Ellie makes marmalade. She sells the marmalade to restaurants in her town. These restaurants are her only source of sales.

Let's assume that a new restaurant opens in town and the owner approaches Ellie and tells her that they would like to buy 500 jars of her marmalade every month. Until this point, Ellie only made 100 jars of marmalade per month. She makes the marmalade in her own kitchen on weekends and distributes them herself. She has very little overhead because she works from home. She doesn't have any employees to pay, and she can keep her full-time teaching job during the week. In order to make an extra 500 jars of marmalade per month, Ellie would have to quit her teaching job, and/or hire several employees. She would have to find someplace else to make the marmalade because her kitchen isn't big enough. Based on the "eggs and basket" common sense rule, would it be wise for Ellie to take the new restaurant up on their offer?

No. Because even if Ellie could make enough profit from selling the extra 500 jars of marmalade to cover her expenses *and* whatever income she would lose by quitting her teaching job, it's not worth the risk. There is no guarantee that the new restaurant will stay in business, or that they will continue to buy 500 jars of marmalade from Ellie every month. Also, if the restaurant owner gets the impression that Ellie depends on the restaurant's business (which she would) the owner might try to pressure her into giving them better deals—deeper discounts. Ellie would be stuck in a dilemma because if she gives in to the owner's demands she wouldn't make the profit she had counted on, but if she refuses—the restaurant could take its business elsewhere. Either way, Ellie would likely go out of business.

Don't become dependent on any one source for a large percentage of your income.

9

Change With the Times

I hope your business will be successful—so successful that you'll be in business many years. So keep in mind that, when it comes to business, if you're doing it the way you did it five years ago, you're probably doing it wrong. You've got to keep up with the times. Be dynamic, not stagnant! Just think about the companies that manufactured wagon wheels—some of these businesses may have been around for hundreds of years, but if they didn't look for new ways to make money when the automobile came along, they'd most likely go broke in a short time.

Many famous companies have been in existence for years, and a major component of that success is that they maintained their quality while changing with the times. Imagine how silly it would be if someone tried to transport their goods using a horse and wagon in this century of airplanes and motor vehicles. Imagine how old-fashioned a company would appear if they wrote business letters by hand, rather than using a computer. Somewhere along the line, companies that existed for dozens of years have had to change the way they do business. And, hopefully, you will continue to adapt the way you do business because this will help your company endure through the years.

Just look at the changes that have occurred within your own lifetime. Do you ever watch reruns of the television programs that were popular when you were a child and laugh at the "crazy" clothes and hairstyles people wore? Well, back then those were *the* styles to wear, just like what's "in" today is *the* thing to wear. Now, imagine if a clothing company was still designing fashions the same way they did back in the 1920s, 1950s, or 1980s—there probably wouldn't be much of a market for their products today.

Also, think of the way the market demographics have changed. For example, when I was a young man, most women were stay-at-home wives and mothers. Advertisements for food, clothing, and household goods were targeted to fit the lifestyles of these women. Today, however, women have a strong presence in the workforce. Ads for food, clothing, and household goods have changed to reflect the needs of the "working woman." Some products have changed as well— for example, there are many more ready-made meals available at the grocery store for today's families than there were in the days when my wife used to cook all the meals for our family. Other products (such as shampoo) have remained virtually the same but the advertising message has changed with the times to reflect the lifestyle of the persons purchasing the product.

Again, you need to base your changes on market conditions, on what your competitors are doing, and on your own budget and time constraints. In fact, it's a good idea to anticipate trends, fads, and technological advancements when deciding what kind of product or service you want to offer. Some services, like offering haircuts or childcare, have changed very little over time. Others, like information technology consulting, change almost daily. The same is true with products. Fashion and technological products constantly change, while other items (like arts and crafts or basic food products) have remained virtually unchanged over the years. Nobody wants to use a computer from the early 1980s or a swimming suit from the 1880s, but we still love good "old-fashioned" apple pie and holiday decorations for our homes.

Just remember that your company should never be stagnant. Maintain the quality, but revitalize! You don't have to completely rebuild your company every few months, but you should be aware of what's going on in the world around you and be ready to change—your product, your advertising, your store decor, your computer system—when the time comes.

10

Needs Versus Wants

When you're deciding what product or service to offer—which one will be most enduring—it's also important to consider whether that product or service will fill a customer's "need" or their "want."

"Needs" are all the things that a person must have in order to live a decent life – food, clothing, and shelter particularly.

"Wants" are all the things that are not necessary to survive in life, but that make life better and more enjoyable. For example, in this country, someone could live quite comfortably in a modest home that has indoor plumbing, electricity, and heat. However, most people like to have homes that are large, or aesthetically pleasing. They *want* a fancy whirlpool bathtub, designer light fixtures, a fireplace for "ambiance" rather than warmth. I'm sure you can think of examples in your own life. For example, a nutritious meal is a "need" because it helps you stay healthy and grow. A candy bar for dessert is a "want"—you could live without it, but it sure does taste good. Shoes are a "need"—fancy designer shoes endorsed by your favorite celebrity are a "want."

Sometimes, it can be profitable to go into business to cater to a "want"—a lot of people are eager to pay money for popular fads or the things that make them feel good. But, for more stability long-term, it's better to go into a business that caters to needs. If times are tough and people don't have a lot of money, they will purchase needs rather than wants. I lived through the Great Depression, I saw many companies that offered wants—luxuries—go out of business in a hurry because people had to spend their few precious dollars on fulfilling basic necessities of life.

11

Business is Hands-On

When it comes to running your business, there is only one person capable of doing the job—*you*. Your business should be "hands-on," meaning that you've got to keep your hands (and eyes) on the business at all times. You have to be in control.

It's easy to keep watch over everything when your business is small and in its early stages. Maybe you will be the only person working in your business at first. But, if your business grows to the point that you start hiring employees, and you begin to delegate and departmentalize the various tasks that you used to do yourself, you've got to be careful. Never get so busy that you can't oversee the entire operation. Never think that you are too important to do the "little things." Those "little" things won't seem so little if they signal the downfall of your company. This is not to say that the people working for you are crooks or inept—chances are they are decent, hard-working people just like you. But the important reality is, it's not their business, it's *yours*. You started it. You know *everything* about it. You are most motivated to see it succeed. Yes, you should listen to other opinions and let people help you but, ultimately, you know what's best for your business.

And always remember to listen to your common sense. If somebody is doing something or saying something that just doesn't make sense to you, listen to yourself—don't just accept their advice because they are an "expert" or supposedly have more knowledge or success than you do.

Years ago, one of the nation's leading drugstore companies hired a new CEO. He was "an expert," "brilliant," he had the "credentials," the "experience." He got the idea that the drugstore ought to begin selling furniture. Wow—a combination drugstore/furniture store! What could be better, he said. But he had not done research to see if anybody else shared his opinion.

When I heard about this, I asked myself: is it common sense to go to a drugstore to buy furniture? No, the two products aren't even related. And probably a lot of people in that guy's company thought it was a ridiculous idea, but they didn't want to say anything to challenge the "expert." So the company tried it. And, of course, the idea of a combination drugstore/furniture store did not catch on with consumers, who still preferred to shop at a drugstore for medicine and a furniture store for furniture and didn't like the idea of the two being mixed. So the company went broke.

So, yes, listen to the opinions of others—never feel that you know everything. Yet, don't go along with something just because it is popular or because someone "important" suggests it. Remember to use your own common sense and look at the overall picture.

12

Inventory

If you have a product-related business, inventory management is another important consideration in your business strategy.

As you probably guessed, inventory management is the practice of managing your inventory. *Good* inventory management means always having enough of what the customer wants to buy without having extra inventory sitting in storage.

Again, it's common sense. If you have $10 and you spend it on a book, you have a book and you no longer have $10. So you can't spend that $10 on dinner, a t-shirt, or a birthday present for your friend. The book might be nice, but if you need to eat dinner, you can't eat the book.

Well, it's the same with business. If you spend $100 on ten books to sell in your bookstore, you no longer have that $100 in cash. You have $100 worth of books that you plan to sell for $20 each. And if people come to your store and buy the ten books right away, that's great, because then not only do you have your initial investment of $100 back, you made an additional $100. And you can use that money to buy more books, or pay your bills, or save for a vacation...

But let's say that, in an entire month, only one person buys only one book. Now you are left with $90 worth of inventory (books), and $20 cash. But you need $100 to pay your bills. Where is that money going to come from? Most likely your electric company and landlord and employee don't want to accept payment in the form of books! Having too much money tied-up in inventory is not a good thing.

Also, look at it this way. The shelf space in your store is limited. There is only room for so many books. And if the shelf space is filled with books nobody buys, that's bad for two reasons. The first reason is the one I already mentioned: you won't have the cash to pay your bills, let alone make any profit for the things you want personally. But there's another problem, too: as long as those unpopular books are on the shelves, you can't try to sell any popular books. There's no money to buy the popular books and no place to put them. So, if you can't sell the books you already have, you've actually lost more than the $90 in the unsold inventory. You also lost the *profit* you could have made by selling the popular books instead.

Again, this comes down to common sense and *knowing your market.*

Research and realize what people want to buy and get them to buy it from you. Would you be wise to promote a picture book of THE NIGHT BEFORE CHRISTMAS in April? How about a Mechanical Engineering textbook at a children's bookstore? Ten thousand copies of a new best-selling novel for your bookstore in Smalltown, population 350? Of course not! Remember our friend with the souvenir shop on the beach in Hawaii? He's selling t-shirts, not wool jackets; postcards, not fine art. Know what people want to buy, and determine how much they would likely buy, then order your inventory accordingly.

13

The Employee, the Employer, and the Entrepreneur

I wrote this book to help you be successful in business. For the most part, the things I have talked about apply to entrepreneurs—the people who will start their own business, rather than going to work for someone else—but managers and employees can use common sense business concepts, too.

Not everyone wants to be an entrepreneur, and not everyone has the personal characteristics to be an entrepreneur—and that's okay. There is nothing wrong with working for someone else, and a lot of people like it. For one thing, there is a different type of risk involved when you work for someone else than if you own your own company.

If you own the business, you own all the good things that may come from it; but you also own all the risks. If business is bad, you are the one who will lose money and sleep. You are the one who will have to find a solution to the problems.

You have to be willing to take those risks.

If you work for another company, you won't have the same type of worries. You might, for example, not be privy to how financially sound your company is, so you might think everything is fine for months or years, only to find out abruptly one day that the company is going out of business or laying people off; but hopefully you can just move on to another company, find another job—provided you have kept up with the times and kept yourself marketable. As an employee, if your company goes broke, you generally won't lose everything.

As an employee, you will probably be limited by how many hours you can work, what decisions you can make, and how much money you can earn. If you own your own business, you determine how many hours you want to work, you make the decisions, and you make all the profits—or take the losses.

Sometimes a person doesn't have the personality characteristics necessary to be a successful entrepreneur. This is not to say that these people are somehow less intelligent or skilled or creative than those who become entrepreneurs, it just means they are more suited to working for someone else. An entrepreneur needs to be self-motivated, responsible, insightful, inventive, and good with people. An entrepreneur must be comfortable with being the final decision maker. And, in many cases, an entrepreneur must be comfortable with managing employees.

If you are going to be a manager, in someone else's company or in your own company, the most important thing to remember is: *learn the personalities of your employees.* If you discover each employee's individual personality, you will know how to best manage that individual employee. And, ultimately, that is the best way to think of the people who work for you: not as a collective (i.e. "my employees") but as unique individuals (i.e. "Jane, Brian, Ann") who join together to help run your business.

Take a moment to think about your friends. I am sure you will see that each friend has a distinct personality and that you most likely behave with each of your friends in a slightly different way. In fact, you may find that you appreciate different qualities in each of your friends (one might be funny, another might be artistic, another might share your favorite hobby). This doesn't mean you are being "fake" in dealing with any particular friend, it just means that you know how to interact with each friend, so that your time with that friend is most enjoyable and agreeable. For example, maybe you like playing chess with one friend and have formed a book club with another friend; but your chess friend doesn't like reading and your literary friend doesn't like chess. It would be pretty ineffective, not to mention annoying to you and your friends, to try to make the literary friend enjoy chess or the chess friend enjoy books. Well, it's the same sort of thing with managing employees. I'll give you an example.

Most people like to be complimented on a job well done. It makes them feel good and encourages them to even greater achievement. So, when I was a manager, I always tried to praise my employees if they did an exceptional job. But I realized that one of the guys didn't respond to praise the way everyone else did. In fact, whenever I told him "good job" he got *worse*. He seemed to think that my compliment meant he was working *too* hard and that he may as well slack off a bit. Of course, I couldn't let that happen. So, I had to stop praising him! I disliked doing that, but it was the only way to get him to improve. So, whenever the employees performed to the level I expected and I told everyone else "good job," I would tell him "You can do better." And he did.

The best way to learn someone's personality is to be observant. Watch them in the interview, during training, and on the job. See how they react to different situations, to you, to customers, to other employees. And, most of all, get them to talk—and be sure that you really listen, not just to their words, but also to their body language.

I've found that the best way to get someone to talk is to stop talking yourself. For example, if someone answers a question you asked, don't comment on their answer right away; nobody likes silence, and if you don't fill the silence, they will—by giving you more information. It's not meant to intimidate them, but to help them reveal more of their personality, their feelings about the situation, and so forth— and this will ultimately help both of you because it's a more genuine communication.

It's important that you be a good listener, not just a good talker. You'd be surprised at how few people are truly good listeners, and how appreciated and respected a good listener really is. Encourage people to feel comfortable talking with you. Show them that you truly listen and you will learn a lot about their personalities that will help you manage them more effectively. But, above all, you have to be honest about it. Always remember that when you discover the best way to manage someone it will not only benefit you (because you get an efficient employee), it will benefit them, too, because they know they have a boss who cares about treating them with the respect and individual attention they deserve. And this makes the business itself stronger.

It's also important that a manager be firm, but fair. Throughout my many years in the business world, I found that people always respect a manager who is firm but fair. While most people want an amiable manager, they also want a manager who enforces rules, who treats everyone equally, and who isn't a pushover. Meanwhile, be sure you aren't too ridgid in your management technique. Always remember that you are not the only employer in the world and, if your employees don't like you, they can quit and work elsewhere. One thing to keep in mind is that you should be careful in how you reprimand employees. Don't get upset with them over trivial matters; this could lower their morale and make them perform poorly. Again, show compassion and understanding; but be sure they know that you stand firm on the issues most important to you and the business.

Another part of the "fairness" factor is that you should be confidential in your dealings with employees. Never use one employee, by name, as an example to other employees—no matter whether the example is a positive or negative one. You can speak in generalities about things you have observed, but don't pinpoint anyone. This way you will be a neutral manager, and no one can accuse you of favoritism.

You've probably heard the expression "honesty is the best policy." Well, I don't think there is a better statement that can be applied to the business world. Whether you are dealing with employees or customers, it is always best to be honest. And by honest I don't just mean that you should be truthful (which you should)—I mean that you should also be sincere, trustworthy, and genuine. Whatever you are talking about, whether it be a product you are trying to sell or a new policy you want your employees to follow, you want your listeners to feel that you mean what you say, and that they can believe you. Once again, this is not part of some elaborate business game; it's not acting. It has to be sincere. People can sense when you're trying to fool them, and they can also sense when you are genuine. And even though being honest is an ethical obligation, it is also good for business. When you have integrity, when people learn that they can trust you, they will be more likely to want to be your employee or customer because they know they will be treated fairly.

14

Salesmanship

We just spent time talking about honesty. Unfortunately, a lot of people think that salespeople are not honest. And, unfortunately, this is true in some cases. But, a lot of salespeople are honest, they really believe in the products/services they sell, and they think that it truly will make the customer's life better if the customer purchases that product/service.

If you decide to work for someone else, hopefully you will work for a company whose product/service you believe in. If you go into business for yourself, chances are you will be marketing a product/service you believe in very much. In either case, customers will sense your sincerity and this will lend credibility to your sales pitch.

What did you think of when I said "sales pitch?" A lot of people have negative thoughts and feelings associated with that term. That's because, often times, salespeople have a pre-scripted sales pitch that they make to every customer, regardless of that customer's needs. This is one of the things that give some salespeople a reputation for being pushy and insincere.

It is wise to know a lot about the product/service you are trying to sell, but you don't want to have a canned sales pitch. Just like with management, the most important key to success in salesmanship is *listening*. Really try to understand what your customer wants, then talk about your product/service in a way that illustrates to the customer that the product/service will meet his/her requirements–but don't try to sell the customer something he/she doesn't truly want. Also, don't try to talk the customer into buying more of something than he/she wants; if the customer says "I'll take five widgets," don't try to sell her a gidget, too—that might make you seem pushy and greedy and then the customer might not buy *anything* from you.

Finally, don't make promises you can't keep. So, be certain that you will honor what you tell your customers. You might not remember what you said if you over-promise, *but they will.*

I remember a restaurant owner who bought quite a lot of coffee from our company. Whenever I would talk with him, he would make notes of our conversation. After we had been doing business for a year, he asked me to come to his office to meet with him. When I got there, I saw all the notes he had taken throughout the year scattered across his desk. He asked me to tell him again the terms and conditions I had given him when we started doing business together. And as I talked, he read his notes. At the end of our meeting he said, "Well, I wanted to see if you followed through on everything you promised; and I see that you have. What you said to me previously is what you say to me now. I figured you couldn't remember lies after one year, but you'd remember the truth. You're an honest guy. And you've made me a loyal customer from here on!"

15

Deciding Which Business to Go Into

Before you start a business, it is important to determine which type of business you should go into. A good starting point would be to examine your own personal strengths (and weaknesses) and knowledge, as well as what you are interested in and excited about.

Think about school subjects for a moment. In all probability, there are certain subjects you like better than others, and there are certain subjects you excel in more than others—and most likely, these are one and the same. For example, if you love the subject of English, you are probably pretty good at it. Oftentimes, the things we like best are the things we do best, or vice versa.

Well, the same is true in business. If there is a particular type of product or service you are most interested in, and knowledgeable about, you will probably do a good job of selling it, and you will be enthusiastic about making your business successful because you love it.

Again, think about school subjects. If you dislike history, you probably won't enjoy telling people about it, and you won't want to spend all your time studying it; but if you love history you will be much more eager to tell your friends about the things you are studying. In fact, you might even enjoy reading about history in your free time, too.

In today's business world, I believe service-related businesses are more likely to succeed as small businesses than product-related businesses. That doesn't mean that you should completely rule out selling a product, if that is what you truly want to do, but certain special concerns exist for people in product-related businesses. For one thing, even if you come up with an original product idea, other businesses can try to make a product that is better or less costly than yours. So, it is important to protect your ideas. For example, books can by copyrighted and inventions can be patented. You will probably need an attorney to help you in this area. Eventually someone will try to compete with you if you are successful.

Many product-related companies rely on price strategies to be competitive. They try to get people to buy their product because theirs is cheaper than a similar product by another company. This is a very dangerous marketing strategy because there comes a point when you just can't sell something any cheaper or you won't be able to cover the costs involved to make the product; so you *lose* money. And if it costs a competitor less money to make the product than it costs you, they will be able to sell it cheaper and you will be out of business—*unless* you have some other incentive for people to buy from you, something for which they are willing to pay extra, for example, outstanding customer service.

This is also the case when you are *selling* products that you buy from a distributor. Perhaps you have seen (or heard of) the movie YOU'VE GOT MAIL. In that movie, Kathleen Kelly (played by Meg Ryan) owns a small bookstore. She loves books and she knows everything about every book she sells so customers love to buy from her because she is so knowledgeable. Meanwhile, Joe Fox (played by Tom Hanks) owns one of the largest bookstore chains in the country and opens a store in the same area where Kathleen Kelly's bookstore is located. Because Joe Fox's company is so huge it can buy thousands of books from publishers at deep discounts, and he can then pass those savings along to his customers. But Kathleen Kelly can't afford to buy large quantities of books from her distributors, so she doesn't receive the deeper discounts and can't sell to her customers at competitive prices. When Kathleen Kelly's customers start buying books from Joe Fox's store, she is forced to close her business because she can't compete with his low prices.

Unfortunately, this happens very often these days. Sometimes, a small "mom and pop" store has a strong enough reputation and customer base to survive, even in the face of big-business competition. But often, especially when the economy is down, people just want their hard-earned money to buy as much as possible, and they are willing to sacrifice quality customer service for low prices.

Again, I am not trying to tell you that you *can't* or *shouldn't* go into a product-related business; I just want you to be aware of the special concerns that go along with running one, even on a small scale.

While you still have to be mindful of your competition if you are in a service-related business, it's a little easier to stay competitive, even against big businesses. Let's contrast our example of the bookseller with an example of a hairstylist.

In the case of the booksellers, if you as a customer want to purchase a new copy of WINNIE THE POOH you are presented with two choices: 1) Go to a small bookseller, receive the best service, and pay cover price, or 2) Go to the discount bookseller, receive less knowledgeable service, and get a discount on the book. Either way, you will own WINNIE THE POOH—the product you wanted is the product you receive.

In the case of a hairstylist, however, a customer may not get exactly what is wanted. If, for example, you would like to have your hair cut in the same style as your favorite movie star, you could go to a hairstylist and tell the hairstylist to style your hair that particular way. You could choose to pay more and go to a well-established hair salon in your area, one where you know the hairstylists have been trained to exacting standards and know all the latest techniques; or, you could choose to go to your friend's sister's cousin's house because you heard she just started cosmetology school and she is giving really inexpensive haircuts. Chances are, you'll get what you pay for. Sure, you will receive a haircut one way or the other—but the less-experienced hairstylist might not be able to give you the look you wanted.

Another advantage to providing a service rather than a product is that with a service *you* can set the rate you charge based on how much you are willing to work for. With a product, you have to cover the costs involved in making/buying the product. For example, if something is broken and you need to hire someone to repair it, the end result should be that the broken item is fixed. No matter how low a rate a repairperson might be willing to charge you, the repairperson will have to fix the broken item. Period. But at least the repairperson has more flexibility in determining his/her rates. Once the cost of tools and materials are covered, the repairperson can choose to work for less than competitors charge if need be, until his/her reputation has been established.

Once again, no matter what kind of service business you work in, customer service is key. If all the repairpersons in your area are able to fix widgets, there has to be a reason people with broken widgets will want *you* to fix them rather than another repairperson. Yes, this could be because you charge less. But remember that it is always in your business's best long-term interests to build an excellent reputation and deliver excellent customer service. Don't base your competitive strategy on price alone.

16

The Other Stuff
You Need to Know

This book is about common sense. I believe common sense is the biggest key to success in business and my goal has been to share with you some of the common sense wisdom I've learned though many, many years in the business world.

Although most things can be learned through observation and experience, some things cannot. However, observation and experience *can* help you determine those areas of business that are *not* common sense but are acquired skills, such as mathematics, accounting, and business law. To learn these subjects, it is important to study a book, take a course, or learn from someone reputable in the field because these concepts are not easily "observable" for most people. We must become acquainted with the principles of mathematics, the rules of accounting, and the numerous and various laws that are in effect.

If you are going to start your own business, you need to know some mathematics—there's no way around that. I'm not saying you have to learn calculus, but you should know basic mathematical concepts and applications. What you learn in high school should be sufficient, although you might want to invest in a business mathematics textbook to help you apply the skills you learn to business issues. Your local college might have some business mathematics texts that you can purchase. Enrolling in a business mathematics course may be helpful so you can ask the instructor questions that might arise during your studies.

It's also wise to know a little about statistics. Even if you don't know how to do much with statistics yourself, you should be aware of how other people manipulate statistics to their benefit.[6]

You should also learn a little bit about accounting. Again, nothing fancy, but the basics of bookkeeping are vital. Many aspects of accounting are common sense (i.e. you want to make more money than you spend). But it is important to learn how to keep accurate and complete records so that you know where your money is coming from and going to, and exactly how much you have. Again, depending upon how much time you have available, you might want to enroll in a community college course on Accounting Fundamentals— that way, if you have questions about how to do things, you will have an instructor to help you. Or, you might just try to locate a basic textbook on accounting and study by yourself.

Finally, make sure that what you are doing is legal. The government has many laws and regulations established for business owners. You have to make sure you have proper permits, that you pay appropriate taxes, that you are following regulations when it comes to employee and customer safety, and so forth. Each type of business comes with its own unique

---

[6] A book that explains this well is HOW TO LIE WITH STATISTICS by Darrell Huff.

set of regulations, so make sure you carefully research those that apply to you. Again, you can start with a college course or textbook on Business Law. You can also talk with other people you know who might have their own businesses—but always keep in mind that some people, innocently or purposely, might not be following all the rules. Always make sure you check with the appropriate governmental agencies so that you know *you* are following the law.

17

There is No "Final Answer"

By now, you have probably realized that there is no absolute final answer when it comes to how to succeed in business. Every person is different, and businesses are made up of people, so every business situation will be different. That's why common sense and observation are so important—draw from past experiences to help guide present ones. Know yourself, know your product, know your market. If you employ common sense, you will know when to turn to others for advice, either through books or school or just in conversation; and you will know when to trust yourself and your instincts to do what's best for your business. No one can tell you exactly what to do for every situation. You have to trust yourself and not simply rely on others to map out your road to success. Yes, it can be a little frightening, a little daunting, but this self-reliance can also be wonderfully invigorating and inspiring.

This book was written to share with you some of my experiences in business, experiences that will be helpful for you to keep in mind as you embark upon your own career. I hope that you will remember this book, not as a guidebook, but rather as a sort of mirror or magnifying glass—one that will help you better see your strengths, weaknesses, and goals and more closely observe the world around you and how business might fit into your future. Hopefully, this book has raised your awareness of some of the possible situations that may arise for you in the business world. More importantly, I hope it has helped you appreciate the significance of *being aware*, of looking at things from multiple perspectives, and of always being ready for change. And I hope it has encouraged you to greet every situation in business with a good measure of common sense.

I wish you happiness and success in your endeavors!

Index

Published by Bluestocking Press

Uncle Eric Books by Richard J. Maybury

UNCLE ERIC TALKS ABOUT PERSONAL, CAREER, AND FINANCIAL SECURITY

WHATEVER HAPPENED TO PENNY CANDY?

WHATEVER HAPPENED TO JUSTICE?

ARE YOU LIBERAL? CONSERVATIVE? OR CONFUSED?

ANCIENT ROME: HOW IT AFFECTS YOU TODAY

EVALUATING BOOKS: WHAT WOULD THOMAS JEFFERSON THINK ABOUT THIS?

THE MONEY MYSTERY

THE CLIPPER SHIP STRATEGY

THE THOUSAND YEAR WAR IN THE MIDEAST

WORLD WAR I: THE REST OF THE STORY

WORLD WAR II: THE REST OF THE STORY

Bluestocking Guides (study guides for the Uncle Eric books)
by Jane A. Williams and/or Kathryn Daniels

Each Study Guide includes some or all of the following:

1) chapter-by-chapter comprehension questions and answers
2) application questions and answers
3) research activities
4) essay assignments
5) thought questions
6) final exam

More Bluestocking Press Titles

LAURA INGALLS WILDER AND ROSE WILDER LANE HISTORICAL TIMETABLE

CAPITALISM FOR KIDS: GROWING UP TO BE YOUR OWN BOSS by Karl Hess

COMMON SENSE BUSINESS FOR KIDS by Kathryn Daniels

ECONOMICS: A FREE MARKET READER edited by Jane Williams & Kathryn Daniels

Order information: Order any of the above by phone or online from:

Bluestocking Press
Phone: 800-959-8586
email: CustomerService@BluestockingPress.com
web site: www.BluestockingPress.com